EQUIPMENT MAINTENANCE

Log book

EQUIPMENT MAINTENANCE LOG BOOK

	Additional Information
Equipment:	
Manufacture:	
Model No:	
Item Location:	
Serial No:	
Purchase Date:	

Date	Time	Maintenance Task / Remarks	Performed By	Cost

Notes:

EQUIPMENT MAINTENANCE LOG BOOK

Equipment:	Additional Information
Manufacture:	
Model No:	
Item Location:	
Serial No:	
Purchase Date:	

Date	Time	Maintenance Task / Remarks	Performed By	Cost

Notes:

EQUIPMENT MAINTENANCE LOG BOOK

Equipment:	Additional Information
Manufacture:	
Model No:	
Item Location:	
Serial No:	
Purchase Date:	

Date	Time	Maintenance Task / Remarks	Performed By	Cost

Notes:

EQUIPMENT MAINTENANCE LOG BOOK

Equipment:	Additional Information
Manufacture:	
Model No:	
Item Location:	
Serial No:	
Purchase Date:	

Date	Time	Maintenance Task / Remarks	Performed By	Cost

Notes:

EQUIPMENT MAINTENANCE LOG BOOK

Equipment:	Additional Information
Manufacture:	
Model No:	
Item Location:	
Serial No:	
Purchase Date:	

Date	Time	Maintenance Task / Remarks	Performed By	Cost

Notes:

EQUIPMENT MAINTENANCE LOG BOOK

Equipment:	Additional Information
Manufacture:	
Model No:	
Item Location:	
Serial No:	
Purchase Date:	

Date	Time	Maintenance Task / Remarks	Performed By	Cost

Notes:

EQUIPMENT MAINTENANCE LOG BOOK

Equipment:	Additional Information
Manufacture:	
Model No:	
Item Location:	
Serial No:	
Purchase Date:	

Date	Time	Maintenance Task / Remarks	Performed By	Cost

Notes:

EQUIPMENT MAINTENANCE LOG BOOK

Equipment:	Additional Information
Manufacture:	
Model No:	
Item Location:	
Serial No:	
Purchase Date:	

Date	Time	Maintenance Task / Remarks	Performed By	Cost

Notes:

EQUIPMENT MAINTENANCE LOG BOOK

Equipment:	Additional Information
Manufacture:	
Model No:	
Item Location:	
Serial No:	
Purchase Date:	

Date	Time	Maintenance Task / Remarks	Performed By	Cost

Notes:

EQUIPMENT MAINTENANCE LOG BOOK

	Additional Information
Equipment:	
Manufacture:	
Model No:	
Item Location:	
Serial No:	
Purchase Date:	

Date	Time	Maintenance Task / Remarks	Performed By	Cost

Notes:

EQUIPMENT MAINTENANCE LOG BOOK

Equipment:	Additional Information
Manufacture:	
Model No:	
Item Location:	
Serial No:	
Purchase Date:	

Date	Time	Maintenance Task / Remarks	Performed By	Cost

Notes:

EQUIPMENT MAINTENANCE LOG BOOK

Equipment:	Additional Information
Manufacture:	
Model No:	
Item Location:	
Serial No:	
Purchase Date:	

Date	Time	Maintenance Task / Remarks	Performed By	Cost

Notes:

EQUIPMENT MAINTENANCE LOG BOOK

Equipment:	Additional Information
Manufacture:	
Model No:	
Item Location:	
Serial No:	
Purchase Date:	

Date	Time	Maintenance Task / Remarks	Performed By	Cost

Notes:

EQUIPMENT MAINTENANCE LOG BOOK

Equipment:	Additional Information
Manufacture:	
Model No:	
Item Location:	
Serial No:	
Purchase Date:	

Date	Time	Maintenance Task / Remarks	Performed By	Cost

Notes:

EQUIPMENT MAINTENANCE LOG BOOK

Equipment:	Additional Information
Manufacture:	
Model No:	
Item Location:	
Serial No:	
Purchase Date:	

Date	Time	Maintenance Task / Remarks	Performed By	Cost

Notes:

EQUIPMENT MAINTENANCE LOG BOOK

Equipment:	Additional Information
Manufacture:	
Model No:	
Item Location:	
Serial No:	
Purchase Date:	

Date	Time	Maintenance Task / Remarks	Performed By	Cost

Notes:

EQUIPMENT MAINTENANCE LOG BOOK

Equipment:	Additional Information
Manufacture:	
Model No:	
Item Location:	
Serial No:	
Purchase Date:	

Date	Time	Maintenance Task / Remarks	Performed By	Cost

Notes:

EQUIPMENT MAINTENANCE LOG BOOK

Equipment:	Additional Information
Manufacture:	
Model No:	
Item Location:	
Serial No:	
Purchase Date:	

Date	Time	Maintenance Task / Remarks	Performed By	Cost

Notes:

EQUIPMENT MAINTENANCE LOG BOOK

Equipment:	Additional Information
Manufacture:	
Model No:	
Item Location:	
Serial No:	
Purchase Date:	

Date	Time	Maintenance Task / Remarks	Performed By	Cost

Notes:

EQUIPMENT MAINTENANCE LOG BOOK

Equipment:	Additional Information
Manufacture:	
Model No:	
Item Location:	
Serial No:	
Purchase Date:	

Date	Time	Maintenance Task / Remarks	Performed By	Cost

Notes:

EQUIPMENT MAINTENANCE LOG BOOK

Equipment:	Additional Information
Manufacture:	
Model No:	
Item Location:	
Serial No:	
Purchase Date:	

Date	Time	Maintenance Task / Remarks	Performed By	Cost

Notes:

EQUIPMENT MAINTENANCE LOG BOOK

Equipment:	Additional Information
Manufacture:	
Model No:	
Item Location:	
Serial No:	
Purchase Date:	

Date	Time	Maintenance Task / Remarks	Performed By	Cost

Notes:

EQUIPMENT MAINTENANCE LOG BOOK

Equipment:	Additional Information
Manufacture:	
Model No:	
Item Location:	
Serial No:	
Purchase Date:	

Date	Time	Maintenance Task / Remarks	Performed By	Cost

Notes:

EQUIPMENT MAINTENANCE LOG BOOK

	Additional Information
Equipment:	
Manufacture:	
Model No:	
Item Location:	
Serial No:	
Purchase Date:	

Date	Time	Maintenance Task / Remarks	Performed By	Cost

Notes:

EQUIPMENT MAINTENANCE LOG BOOK

Equipment:	Additional Information
Manufacture:	
Model No:	
Item Location:	
Serial No:	
Purchase Date:	

Date	Time	Maintenance Task / Remarks	Performed By	Cost

Notes:

EQUIPMENT MAINTENANCE LOG BOOK

Equipment:	Additional Information
Manufacture:	
Model No:	
Item Location:	
Serial No:	
Purchase Date:	

Date	Time	Maintenance Task / Remarks	Performed By	Cost

Notes:

EQUIPMENT MAINTENANCE LOG BOOK

Equipment:	Additional Information
Manufacture:	
Model No:	
Item Location:	
Serial No:	
Purchase Date:	

Date	Time	Maintenance Task / Remarks	Performed By	Cost

Notes:

EQUIPMENT MAINTENANCE LOG BOOK

Equipment:	Additional Information
Manufacture:	
Model No:	
Item Location:	
Serial No:	
Purchase Date:	

Date	Time	Maintenance Task / Remarks	Performed By	Cost

Notes:

EQUIPMENT MAINTENANCE LOG BOOK

Equipment:	Additional Information
Manufacture:	
Model No:	
Item Location:	
Serial No:	
Purchase Date:	

Date	Time	Maintenance Task / Remarks	Performed By	Cost

Notes:

EQUIPMENT MAINTENANCE LOG BOOK

	Additional Information
Equipment:	
Manufacture:	
Model No:	
Item Location:	
Serial No:	
Purchase Date:	

Date	Time	Maintenance Task / Remarks	Performed By	Cost

Notes:

EQUIPMENT MAINTENANCE LOG BOOK

	Additional Information
Equipment:	
Manufacture:	
Model No:	
Item Location:	
Serial No:	
Purchase Date:	

Date	Time	Maintenance Task / Remarks	Performed By	Cost

Notes:

EQUIPMENT MAINTENANCE LOG BOOK

Equipment:	Additional Information
Manufacture:	
Model No:	
Item Location:	
Serial No:	
Purchase Date:	

Date	Time	Maintenance Task / Remarks	Performed By	Cost

Notes:

EQUIPMENT MAINTENANCE LOG BOOK

	Additional Information
Equipment:	
Manufacture:	
Model No:	
Item Location:	
Serial No:	
Purchase Date:	

Date	Time	Maintenance Task / Remarks	Performed By	Cost

Notes:

EQUIPMENT MAINTENANCE LOG BOOK

Equipment:	Additional Information
Manufacture:	
Model No:	
Item Location:	
Serial No:	
Purchase Date:	

Date	Time	Maintenance Task / Remarks	Performed By	Cost

Notes:

EQUIPMENT MAINTENANCE LOG BOOK

	Additional Information
Equipment:	
Manufacture:	
Model No:	
Item Location:	
Serial No:	
Purchase Date:	

Date	Time	Maintenance Task / Remarks	Performed By	Cost

Notes:

EQUIPMENT MAINTENANCE LOG BOOK

Equipment:	Additional Information
Manufacture:	
Model No:	
Item Location:	
Serial No:	
Purchase Date:	

Date	Time	Maintenance Task / Remarks	Performed By	Cost

Notes:

EQUIPMENT MAINTENANCE LOG BOOK

Equipment:	Additional Information
Manufacture:	
Model No:	
Item Location:	
Serial No:	
Purchase Date:	

Date	Time	Maintenance Task / Remarks	Performed By	Cost

Notes:

EQUIPMENT MAINTENANCE LOG BOOK

Equipment:	Additional Information
Manufacture:	
Model No:	
Item Location:	
Serial No:	
Purchase Date:	

Date	Time	Maintenance Task / Remarks	Performed By	Cost

Notes:

EQUIPMENT MAINTENANCE LOG BOOK

Equipment:	Additional Information
Manufacture:	
Model No:	
Item Location:	
Serial No:	
Purchase Date:	

Date	Time	Maintenance Task / Remarks	Performed By	Cost

Notes:

EQUIPMENT MAINTENANCE LOG BOOK

Equipment:	Additional Information
Manufacture:	
Model No:	
Item Location:	
Serial No:	
Purchase Date:	

Date	Time	Maintenance Task / Remarks	Performed By	Cost

Notes:

EQUIPMENT MAINTENANCE LOG BOOK

	Additional Information
Equipment:	
Manufacture:	
Model No:	
Item Location:	
Serial No:	
Purchase Date:	

Date	Time	Maintenance Task / Remarks	Performed By	Cost

Notes:

EQUIPMENT MAINTENANCE LOG BOOK

Equipment:	Additional Information
Manufacture:	
Model No:	
Item Location:	
Serial No:	
Purchase Date:	

Date	Time	Maintenance Task / Remarks	Performed By	Cost

Notes:

EQUIPMENT MAINTENANCE LOG BOOK

	Additional Information
Equipment:	
Manufacture:	
Model No:	
Item Location:	
Serial No:	
Purchase Date:	

Date	Time	Maintenance Task / Remarks	Performed By	Cost

Notes:

EQUIPMENT MAINTENANCE LOG BOOK

Equipment:	Additional Information
Manufacture:	
Model No:	
Item Location:	
Serial No:	
Purchase Date:	

Date	Time	Maintenance Task / Remarks	Performed By	Cost

Notes:

EQUIPMENT MAINTENANCE LOG BOOK

Equipment:	Additional Information
Manufacture:	
Model No:	
Item Location:	
Serial No:	
Purchase Date:	

Date	Time	Maintenance Task / Remarks	Performed By	Cost

Notes:

EQUIPMENT MAINTENANCE LOG BOOK

	Additional Information
Equipment:	
Manufacture:	
Model No:	
Item Location:	
Serial No:	
Purchase Date:	

Date	Time	Maintenance Task / Remarks	Performed By	Cost

Notes:

EQUIPMENT MAINTENANCE LOG BOOK

Equipment:	Additional Information
Manufacture:	
Model No:	
Item Location:	
Serial No:	
Purchase Date:	

Date	Time	Maintenance Task / Remarks	Performed By	Cost

Notes:

EQUIPMENT MAINTENANCE LOG BOOK

Equipment:	Additional Information
Manufacture:	
Model No:	
Item Location:	
Serial No:	
Purchase Date:	

Date	Time	Maintenance Task / Remarks	Performed By	Cost

Notes:

EQUIPMENT MAINTENANCE LOG BOOK

Equipment:	Additional Information
Manufacture:	
Model No:	
Item Location:	
Serial No:	
Purchase Date:	

Date	Time	Maintenance Task / Remarks	Performed By	Cost

Notes:

EQUIPMENT MAINTENANCE LOG BOOK

	Additional Information
Equipment:	
Manufacture:	
Model No:	
Item Location:	
Serial No:	
Purchase Date:	

Date	Time	Maintenance Task / Remarks	Performed By	Cost

Notes:

EQUIPMENT MAINTENANCE LOG BOOK

Equipment:	Additional Information
Manufacture:	
Model No:	
Item Location:	
Serial No:	
Purchase Date:	

Date	Time	Maintenance Task / Remarks	Performed By	Cost

Notes:

EQUIPMENT MAINTENANCE LOG BOOK

	Additional Information
Equipment:	
Manufacture:	
Model No:	
Item Location:	
Serial No:	
Purchase Date:	

Date	Time	Maintenance Task / Remarks	Performed By	Cost

Notes:

EQUIPMENT MAINTENANCE LOG BOOK

	Additional Information
Equipment:	
Manufacture:	
Model No:	
Item Location:	
Serial No:	
Purchase Date:	

Date	Time	Maintenance Task / Remarks	Performed By	Cost

Notes:

EQUIPMENT MAINTENANCE LOG BOOK

	Additional Information
Equipment:	
Manufacture:	
Model No:	
Item Location:	
Serial No:	
Purchase Date:	

Date	Time	Maintenance Task / Remarks	Performed By	Cost

Notes:

EQUIPMENT MAINTENANCE LOG BOOK

	Additional Information
Equipment:	
Manufacture:	
Model No:	
Item Location:	
Serial No:	
Purchase Date:	

Date	Time	Maintenance Task / Remarks	Performed By	Cost

Notes:

EQUIPMENT MAINTENANCE LOG BOOK

Equipment:	**Additional Information**
Manufacture:	
Model No:	
Item Location:	
Serial No:	
Purchase Date:	

Date	Time	Maintenance Task / Remarks	Performed By	Cost

Notes:

EQUIPMENT MAINTENANCE LOG BOOK

	Additional Information
Equipment:	
Manufacture:	
Model No:	
Item Location:	
Serial No:	
Purchase Date:	

Date	Time	Maintenance Task / Remarks	Performed By	Cost

Notes:

EQUIPMENT MAINTENANCE LOG BOOK

Equipment:	Additional Information
Manufacture:	
Model No:	
Item Location:	
Serial No:	
Purchase Date:	

Date	Time	Maintenance Task / Remarks	Performed By	Cost

Notes:

EQUIPMENT MAINTENANCE LOG BOOK

	Additional Information
Equipment:	
Manufacture:	
Model No:	
Item Location:	
Serial No:	
Purchase Date:	

Date	Time	Maintenance Task / Remarks	Performed By	Cost

Notes:

EQUIPMENT MAINTENANCE LOG BOOK

Equipment:	Additional Information
Manufacture:	
Model No:	
Item Location:	
Serial No:	
Purchase Date:	

Date	Time	Maintenance Task / Remarks	Performed By	Cost

Notes:

EQUIPMENT MAINTENANCE LOG BOOK

Equipment:	Additional Information
Manufacture:	
Model No:	
Item Location:	
Serial No:	
Purchase Date:	

Date	Time	Maintenance Task / Remarks	Performed By	Cost

Notes:

EQUIPMENT MAINTENANCE LOG BOOK

Equipment:	Additional Information
Manufacture:	
Model No:	
Item Location:	
Serial No:	
Purchase Date:	

Date	Time	Maintenance Task / Remarks	Performed By	Cost

Notes:

EQUIPMENT MAINTENANCE LOG BOOK

Equipment:	Additional Information
Manufacture:	
Model No:	
Item Location:	
Serial No:	
Purchase Date:	

Date	Time	Maintenance Task / Remarks	Performed By	Cost

Notes:

EQUIPMENT MAINTENANCE LOG BOOK

Equipment:	Additional Information
Manufacture:	
Model No:	
Item Location:	
Serial No:	
Purchase Date:	

Date	Time	Maintenance Task / Remarks	Performed By	Cost

Notes:

EQUIPMENT MAINTENANCE LOG BOOK

Equipment:	Additional Information
Manufacture:	
Model No:	
Item Location:	
Serial No:	
Purchase Date:	

Date	Time	Maintenance Task / Remarks	Performed By	Cost

Notes:

EQUIPMENT MAINTENANCE LOG BOOK

Equipment:	Additional Information
Manufacture:	
Model No:	
Item Location:	
Serial No:	
Purchase Date:	

Date	Time	Maintenance Task / Remarks	Performed By	Cost

Notes:

EQUIPMENT MAINTENANCE LOG BOOK

	Additional Information
Equipment:	
Manufacture:	
Model No:	
Item Location:	
Serial No:	
Purchase Date:	

Date	Time	Maintenance Task / Remarks	Performed By	Cost

Notes:

EQUIPMENT MAINTENANCE LOG BOOK

Equipment:	Additional Information
Manufacture:	
Model No:	
Item Location:	
Serial No:	
Purchase Date:	

Date	Time	Maintenance Task / Remarks	Performed By	Cost

Notes:

EQUIPMENT MAINTENANCE LOG BOOK

	Additional Information
Equipment:	
Manufacture:	
Model No:	
Item Location:	
Serial No:	
Purchase Date:	

Date	Time	Maintenance Task / Remarks	Performed By	Cost

Notes:

EQUIPMENT MAINTENANCE LOG BOOK

Equipment:	Additional Information
Manufacture:	
Model No:	
Item Location:	
Serial No:	
Purchase Date:	

Date	Time	Maintenance Task / Remarks	Performed By	Cost

Notes:

EQUIPMENT MAINTENANCE LOG BOOK

Equipment:	Additional Information
Manufacture:	
Model No:	
Item Location:	
Serial No:	
Purchase Date:	

Date	Time	Maintenance Task / Remarks	Performed By	Cost

Notes:

EQUIPMENT MAINTENANCE LOG BOOK

Equipment:	Additional Information
Manufacture:	
Model No:	
Item Location:	
Serial No:	
Purchase Date:	

Date	Time	Maintenance Task / Remarks	Performed By	Cost

Notes:

EQUIPMENT MAINTENANCE LOG BOOK

Equipment:	Additional Information
Manufacture:	
Model No:	
Item Location:	
Serial No:	
Purchase Date:	

Date	Time	Maintenance Task / Remarks	Performed By	Cost

Notes:

EQUIPMENT MAINTENANCE LOG BOOK

Equipment:	Additional Information
Manufacture:	
Model No:	
Item Location:	
Serial No:	
Purchase Date:	

Date	Time	Maintenance Task / Remarks	Performed By	Cost

Notes:

EQUIPMENT MAINTENANCE LOG BOOK

Equipment:	Additional Information
Manufacture:	
Model No:	
Item Location:	
Serial No:	
Purchase Date:	

Date	Time	Maintenance Task / Remarks	Performed By	Cost

Notes:

EQUIPMENT MAINTENANCE LOG BOOK

Equipment:	Additional Information
Manufacture:	
Model No:	
Item Location:	
Serial No:	
Purchase Date:	

Date	Time	Maintenance Task / Remarks	Performed By	Cost

Notes:

EQUIPMENT MAINTENANCE LOG BOOK

Equipment:	Additional Information
Manufacture:	
Model No:	
Item Location:	
Serial No:	
Purchase Date:	

Date	Time	Maintenance Task / Remarks	Performed By	Cost

Notes:

EQUIPMENT MAINTENANCE LOG BOOK

Equipment:	Additional Information
Manufacture:	
Model No:	
Item Location:	
Serial No:	
Purchase Date:	

Date	Time	Maintenance Task / Remarks	Performed By	Cost

Notes:

EQUIPMENT MAINTENANCE LOG BOOK

	Additional Information
Equipment:	
Manufacture:	
Model No:	
Item Location:	
Serial No:	
Purchase Date:	

Date	Time	Maintenance Task / Remarks	Performed By	Cost

Notes:

EQUIPMENT MAINTENANCE LOG BOOK

Equipment:	Additional Information
Manufacture:	
Model No:	
Item Location:	
Serial No:	
Purchase Date:	

Date	Time	Maintenance Task / Remarks	Performed By	Cost

Notes:

EQUIPMENT MAINTENANCE LOG BOOK

Equipment:	Additional Information
Manufacture:	
Model No:	
Item Location:	
Serial No:	
Purchase Date:	

Date	Time	Maintenance Task / Remarks	Performed By	Cost

Notes:

EQUIPMENT MAINTENANCE LOG BOOK

Equipment:	Additional Information
Manufacture:	
Model No:	
Item Location:	
Serial No:	
Purchase Date:	

Date	Time	Maintenance Task / Remarks	Performed By	Cost

Notes:

EQUIPMENT MAINTENANCE LOG BOOK

Equipment:	Additional Information
Manufacture:	
Model No:	
Item Location:	
Serial No:	
Purchase Date:	

Date	Time	Maintenance Task / Remarks	Performed By	Cost

Notes:

EQUIPMENT MAINTENANCE LOG BOOK

	Additional Information
Equipment:	
Manufacture:	
Model No:	
Item Location:	
Serial No:	
Purchase Date:	

Date	Time	Maintenance Task / Remarks	Performed By	Cost

Notes:

EQUIPMENT MAINTENANCE LOG BOOK

Equipment:	Additional Information
Manufacture:	
Model No:	
Item Location:	
Serial No:	
Purchase Date:	

Date	Time	Maintenance Task / Remarks	Performed By	Cost

Notes:

EQUIPMENT MAINTENANCE LOG BOOK

	Additional Information
Equipment:	
Manufacture:	
Model No:	
Item Location:	
Serial No:	
Purchase Date:	

Date	Time	Maintenance Task / Remarks	Performed By	Cost

Notes:

EQUIPMENT MAINTENANCE LOG BOOK

	Additional Information
Equipment:	
Manufacture:	
Model No:	
Item Location:	
Serial No:	
Purchase Date:	

Date	Time	Maintenance Task / Remarks	Performed By	Cost

Notes:

EQUIPMENT MAINTENANCE LOG BOOK

Equipment:	Additional Information
Manufacture:	
Model No:	
Item Location:	
Serial No:	
Purchase Date:	

Date	Time	Maintenance Task / Remarks	Performed By	Cost

Notes:

EQUIPMENT MAINTENANCE LOG BOOK

Equipment:	Additional Information
Manufacture:	
Model No:	
Item Location:	
Serial No:	
Purchase Date:	

Date	Time	Maintenance Task / Remarks	Performed By	Cost

Notes:

EQUIPMENT MAINTENANCE LOG BOOK

Equipment:	Additional Information
Manufacture:	
Model No:	
Item Location:	
Serial No:	
Purchase Date:	

Date	Time	Maintenance Task / Remarks	Performed By	Cost

Notes:

EQUIPMENT MAINTENANCE LOG BOOK

Equipment:	Additional Information
Manufacture:	
Model No:	
Item Location:	
Serial No:	
Purchase Date:	

Date	Time	Maintenance Task / Remarks	Performed By	Cost

Notes:

EQUIPMENT MAINTENANCE LOG BOOK

	Additional Information
Equipment:	
Manufacture:	
Model No:	
Item Location:	
Serial No:	
Purchase Date:	

Date	Time	Maintenance Task / Remarks	Performed By	Cost

Notes:

EQUIPMENT MAINTENANCE LOG BOOK

	Additional Information
Equipment:	
Manufacture:	
Model No:	
Item Location:	
Serial No:	
Purchase Date:	

Date	Time	Maintenance Task / Remarks	Performed By	Cost

Notes:

EQUIPMENT MAINTENANCE LOG BOOK

	Additional Information
Equipment:	
Manufacture:	
Model No:	
Item Location:	
Serial No:	
Purchase Date:	

Date	Time	Maintenance Task / Remarks	Performed By	Cost

Notes:

EQUIPMENT MAINTENANCE LOG BOOK

Equipment:	Additional Information
Manufacture:	
Model No:	
Item Location:	
Serial No:	
Purchase Date:	

Date	Time	Maintenance Task / Remarks	Performed By	Cost

Notes:

EQUIPMENT MAINTENANCE LOG BOOK

Equipment:	Additional Information
Manufacture:	
Model No:	
Item Location:	
Serial No:	
Purchase Date:	

Date	Time	Maintenance Task / Remarks	Performed By	Cost

Notes:

EQUIPMENT MAINTENANCE LOG BOOK

	Additional Information
Equipment:	
Manufacture:	
Model No:	
Item Location:	
Serial No:	
Purchase Date:	

Date	Time	Maintenance Task / Remarks	Performed By	Cost

Notes:

EQUIPMENT MAINTENANCE LOG BOOK

	Additional Information
Equipment:	
Manufacture:	
Model No:	
Item Location:	
Serial No:	
Purchase Date:	

Date	Time	Maintenance Task / Remarks	Performed By	Cost

Notes:

EQUIPMENT MAINTENANCE LOG BOOK

	Additional Information
Equipment:	
Manufacture:	
Model No:	
Item Location:	
Serial No:	
Purchase Date:	

Date	Time	Maintenance Task / Remarks	Performed By	Cost

Notes:

EQUIPMENT MAINTENANCE LOG BOOK

Equipment:	Additional Information
Manufacture:	
Model No:	
Item Location:	
Serial No:	
Purchase Date:	

Date	Time	Maintenance Task / Remarks	Performed By	Cost

Notes:

EQUIPMENT MAINTENANCE LOG BOOK

	Additional Information
Equipment:	
Manufacture:	
Model No:	
Item Location:	
Serial No:	
Purchase Date:	

Date	Time	Maintenance Task / Remarks	Performed By	Cost

Notes:

EQUIPMENT MAINTENANCE LOG BOOK

	Additional Information
Equipment:	
Manufacture:	
Model No:	
Item Location:	
Serial No:	
Purchase Date:	

Date	Time	Maintenance Task / Remarks	Performed By	Cost

Notes:

EQUIPMENT MAINTENANCE LOG BOOK

Equipment:	Additional Information
Manufacture:	
Model No:	
Item Location:	
Serial No:	
Purchase Date:	

Date	Time	Maintenance Task / Remarks	Performed By	Cost

Notes:

EQUIPMENT MAINTENANCE LOG BOOK

Equipment:	Additional Information
Manufacture:	
Model No:	
Item Location:	
Serial No:	
Purchase Date:	

Date	Time	Maintenance Task / Remarks	Performed By	Cost

Notes:

EQUIPMENT MAINTENANCE LOG BOOK

Equipment:	Additional Information
Manufacture:	
Model No:	
Item Location:	
Serial No:	
Purchase Date:	

Date	Time	Maintenance Task / Remarks	Performed By	Cost

Notes:

EQUIPMENT MAINTENANCE LOG BOOK

Equipment:	Additional Information
Manufacture:	
Model No:	
Item Location:	
Serial No:	
Purchase Date:	

Date	Time	Maintenance Task / Remarks	Performed By	Cost

Notes:

EQUIPMENT MAINTENANCE LOG BOOK

Equipment:	Additional Information
Manufacture:	
Model No:	
Item Location:	
Serial No:	
Purchase Date:	

Date	Time	Maintenance Task / Remarks	Performed By	Cost

Notes:

Made in the USA
Las Vegas, NV
10 September 2026

54500206R00063